# 100 DAYS *with God*

by

Jeff Hendley

"It is not its practical activities that are the strength of this Bible Training College, its whole strength lies in the fact that here you are put into soak before God. You have no idea of where God is going to engineer your circumstances, no knowledge of what strain is going to be put on you either at home or abroad, and if you waste your time in over-active energies instead of getting into soak on the great fundamental truths of God's Redemption, you will snap when the strain comes; but if this time of soaking before God is being spent in getting rooted and grounded in God on the unpractical line, you will remain true to Him whatever happens."
Oswald Chambers, *My Utmost for His Highest.*

Library of Congress
Control Number: 2005900526

ISBN 0-9762014-0-2

Published by L'Edge Press
A division of Upside Down Ministries, Inc.
Boone, North Carolina

# Translations

I have chosen to use various translations and paraphrases to help in the reading and understanding of these passages. If you have a favorite translation, then just turn to the passage in your Bible and read it from that translation.

The Old Testament was written in Hebrew and the New Testament was written in Greek. In fact, the Greek language of the New Testament was the "market" language of that time. This means it was the street language or the everyday language that the people used to speak to one another.

Therefore, it helps us to understand what the Bible is saying when we take the original Hebrew and Greek and translate it into our everyday language that we use to communicate. These various translations in this journal are a reflection of the translations that have been done over the past decades.

# Introduction

God invites us into a personal relationship with Himself. Just think! We can have a personal relationship with the God of creation. *It is His idea!*

When Jesus chose His twelve disciples, He made a statement that sheds light on this invitation to a relationship, "*Jesus went up on a mountainside and called to him those he wanted and they came to him...that they might be with him.*" Mark 3:13-14, NIV

In the book of Acts, Peter and John had gotten into a bit of trouble for talking about Jesus after He had died and ascended to Heaven. They also performed a miracle and healed a man crippled for years. Of course, the religious leaders did not take this kindly, so they had Peter and John put into prison. The next day they were dragged into court to testify before all the religious biggies. Listen to what was recorded after they spoke, "*When they saw the courage of Peter and John and realized that they were unschooled, ordinary men, they were astonished and they took note that these men had been with Jesus.*" Acts 4:13, NIV

The unbelievable reality of this relationship is that God wants us to be with Him. He invites us. We do not have to force it. We do not have to do anything to be invited. We are welcomed into God's presence by His invitation. Naturally, the focal point of our lives should be this relationship with God.

> "*Jesus answered, 'Love the Lord your God with all your heart, all your soul, and all your mind. This is the first and most important command.'*
> *And the second command is like the first: Love your neighbor as you love yourself. All the law and the writings of the prophets depend on these two commands.*" Matthew 22:37-40 NCV

Life is all about relationships. Relationships with those around us. A relationship with our own selves. And a relationship with God. Since God is Spirit, this relationship takes on a tad bit of difference.

*"Human life comes from the human parents, but spiritual life comes from the Spirit."...."God is spirit, and those who worship him must worship in spirit and truth."* John 3:6, John 4:24 NCV

The spiritual world is as real as the physical world. But we are not used to dealing with spiritual things so we have to focus a bit more if we are to have a "spiritual relationship" with God.

If we want to pursue this relationship with God we can do so just like we would pursue any relationship that is meaningful. It will take time, energy, and commitment—all geared to getting to know each other.

*100 Days with God* is a tool. It is a tool to help establish a habit of spending a few moments with God during the day. It is designed to bring us into direct contact with the words God has spoken.

There are two assumptions that are being made before starting to use *100 Days with God*:

1. That 2 Corinthians 5:17-18 is a reality in our lives:

   *"For if a person is in Christ he becomesa new person altogether—the past is finished and gone, everything has become fresh and new. All this is God's doing..."* Phillips

2. That there is a desire to have a close relationship with God.

Below are a few hints that will better prepare us for our time with God:

1. Find a place where you can be alone and quiet.

2. Find a time where you can spend a few moments with God. It can be anytime: morning, mid-morning, afternoon, evening, etc.

3. Be consistent but do not get hung up on the "everyday" notion. It would be great if you established a daily pattern but that's not important right now. *100 Days with God* is designed so you can go at your own pace and when you want to get away for a few minutes.

4. It would help to have some type of plan while you are alone and quiet. Here are a few suggestions:

• Items needed:
  - pen
  - Bible
  - *100 Days with God* booklet

**• The Plan**

1) **Read.** Read through the verses at the top of the page. You may want to turn to the verses in your Bible and read more—before and after the verses.

> Deuteronomy 17:19
> *And it shall be with him, and he shall read in it all the days of his life, that he may learn to fear the LORD his God by keeping all the words of this law and these statutes, and doing them...*ESV

2) **Listen.** Listen to the words you are reading. Listen to what these words are saying about the people they are written to and about.

> Matthew 17:5
> *While Peter was still speaking, the shadow of a bright cloud passed over them. From the cloud a voice said, "This is my own dear Son, and I am pleased with him. Listen to what he says!"* CEV

3) **Think.** Think about these words and what they mean. Use the questions—who, what, where, when, why, how—to help pry open these words to reveal the meaning. Someone once said, "Questions are like crowbars, they pry open the truth."

> Philippians 4:8
> *For the rest, brethren, whatever is true, whatever is worthy of reverence and is honorable and seemly, whatever is just, whatever is pure, whatever is lovely and lovable, whatever is kind and winsome and gracious, if there is any virtue and excellence, if there is anything worthy of praise, think on and weigh and take account of these things [fix your minds on them].* AMP

4) **Talk/Pray.** Talk to God about what you are reading, what is happening in your life and about your day. God

> "wants to be included in every activity, every conversation, every problem, and even every thought. You can carry on a continuous, open-ended conversation with him throughout your day, talking to him about whatever you are doing or thinking at the moment." (Warren, pg. 87)

> Jeremiah 33:3
> *Call to me and I will answer you, and will tell you great and hidden things that you have not known.* ESV

5) **Dream.** Ephesians 3:20 says, " *God can do anything, you know—far more than you could ever imagine or guess or request in your wildest dreams! He does it not by pushing us around but by working within us, his Spirit deeply and gently within us.*" (MSG) We cannot out think, out ask, or out dream God. Use this time to reflect on your dreams for your life. A professor I once had asked this question, "What dreams do you dream for God?"

6) **Write.** Write down your thoughts. Keep a simple journal of this time you spend with God. Writing helps to crystallize your thoughts and feelings.

> Psalm 102:18
> *Write this down for the next generation so people not yet born will praise GOD.* MSG

Oswald Chambers, *My Utmost for His Highest*, is a terrific devotional. I have listed several quotes from this book so you can read some of the things he said over 100 years ago.

> "It is not practical activities that are the strength of this Training College...its whole strength lies in the fact you are put here to soak before God...but if this time of soaking before God is being spent in getting rooted and grounded in God...you will remain true to Him whatever happens."

> "Have I a personal history with Jesus Christ? The one sign of discipleship is intimate connection with Him, a knowledge of Jesus Christ which nothing can shake."

> "The measure of the worth of our public activity for God is private and profound communion we have with Him...We have to pitch our tents where we shall always have quiet times with God, however noisy our times with the world may be."

> "There is nothing there apart from the personal relationship. Paul was devoted to a Person not a cause. He was absolutely Jesus Christ's, he saw nothing else, he lived for nothing else."

> "If you want to be of use to God, get rightly related to Jesus Christ and He will make you of use unconsciously every minute you live."

> "It is the innermost of the innermost that reveals the power of life...The central thing about the Kingdom of Jesus Christ is a personal relationship to Himself, not public usefulness to men...but if this time of soaking before God is being spent rooted and grounded in God...you will remain true to him no matter what happens."

> "The whole discipline of life is to enable us to enter into this closest relationship with Jesus Christ...When once we get intimate with Jesus we are never lonely, we never need sympathy, we can pour out all the time...."

My prayer for each of us is that this time of "soaking before God" will enable us to enjoy a personal, intimate relationship with Jesus Christ.

# 100 DAYS *with God*

Day 1 Date: ____________

**Genesis 1:1**

In the beginning God (prepared, formed, fashioned, and) created the heavens and the earth. AMP

Read...Listen...Think...Talk/Pray...Dream...Write.

Day 2 Date: ____________

**Matthew 6:33**
But seek first his kingdom and his righteousness, and all these things will be given to you as well. NIV

Read...Listen...Think...Talk/Pray...Dream...Write.

Day 3 Date: ____________

**Matthew 7:7, 8**

Keep on asking, and you will be given what you ask for. Keep on looking, and you will find. Keep on knocking, and the door will be opened. For everyone who asks, receives. Everyone who seeks, finds. And the door is opened to everyone who knocks. NLT

Read…Listen…Think…Talk/Pray…Dream…Write.

Day 4 Date: ____________

**Joshua 1:5, 8-9**

No man shall be able to stand before you all the days of your life. Just as I was with Moses, so I will be with you. I will not leave you or forsake you...This Book of the Law shall not depart from your mouth, but you shall meditate on it day and night, so that you may be careful to do according to all that is written in it. For then you will make your way prosperous, and then you will have good success. Have I not commanded you? Be strong and courageous. Do not be frightened, and do not be dismayed, for the LORD your God is with you wherever you go. ESV

Read...Listen...Think...Talk/Pray...Dream...Write.

Day 5 Date: ____________

**Matthew 7:12**

Here is a simple, rule-of-thumb guide for behavior: Ask yourself what you want people to do for you, then grab the initiative and do it for them. Add up God's Law and Prophets and this is what you get. MSG

Read...Listen...Think...Talk/Pray...Dream...Write.

Day 6 Date: ____________

**Mark 1:35**

Very early the next morning, Jesus got up and went to a place where he could be alone and pray. CEV

Read…Listen…Think…Talk/Pray…Dream…Write.

Day 7 Date: ____________

**2 Samuel 22:20-26**

He stood me up on a wide-open field; I stood there saved—surprised to be loved! GOD made my life complete when I placed all the pieces before him. When I cleaned up my act, he gave me a fresh start. Indeed, I've kept alert to GOD's ways; I haven't taken God for granted. Every day I review the ways he works, I try not to miss a trick. I feel put back together, and I'm watching my step. GOD rewrote the text of my life when I opened the book of my heart to his eyes. You stick by people who stick with you, you're straight with people who're straight with you.... MSG

Read...Listen...Think...Talk/Pray...Dream...Write.

Day 8 Date: ____________

**Luke 2:52**
And Jesus increased in wisdom and stature, and in favour with God and man. KJV

Read…Listen…Think…Talk/Pray…Dream…Write.

Day 9 Date: ____________

**Matthew 11:28-30**

"Are you tired? Worn out? Burned out on religion? Come to me. Get away with me and you'll recover your life. I'll show you how to take a real rest. Walk with me and work with me—watch how I do it. Learn the unforced rhythms of grace. I won't lay anything heavy or ill-fitting on you. Keep company with me and you'll learn to live freely and lightly." MSG

Read...Listen...Think...Talk/Pray...Dream...Write.

Day 10 Date: ____________

**1 Chronicles 29:10-13**

Therefore David blessed the LORD before all the assembly; and David said: Blessed are You, LORD God of Israel, our Father, forever and ever. Yours, O LORD, is the greatness,

The power and the glory,
The victory and the majesty;
For all that is in heaven and in earth is Yours;
Yours is the kingdom, O LORD,
And You are exalted as head over all.
Both riches and honor come from You,
And You reign over all.
In Your hand is power and might;
In Your hand it is to make great
And to give strength to all.
Now therefore, our God,
We thank You
And praise Your glorious name. NKJV

Read…Listen…Think…Talk/Pray…Dream…Write.

Day 11 Date: ____________

**Matthew 18:19-20**

I promise that when any two of you on earth agree about something you are praying for, my Father in heaven will do it for you. Whenever two or three of you come together in my name, I am there with you. CEV

Read…Listen…Think…Talk/Pray…Dream…Write.

Day 12 Date: ____________

**Matthew 22:37-40**

And He replied to him, You shall love the Lord your God with all your heart and with all your soul and with all your mind (intellect). This is the great (most important, principal) and first commandment. And a second is like it: You shall love your neighbor as [you do] yourself. These two commandments sum up and upon them depend all the Law and the Prophets. AMP

Read…Listen…Think…Talk/Pray…Dream…Write.

Day 13 Date: ____________

**1 Chronicles 29:14**

But who am I, and who are my people, that we could give anything to you? Everything we have has come from you, and we give you only what you have already given us! NLT

Read...Listen...Think...Talk/Pray...Dream...Write.

Day 14 Date: ____________

**John 1:1-2**

In the beginning was the one who is called the Word.
The Word was with God and was truly God.
From the very beginning the Word was with God. CEV

Read...Listen...Think...Talk/Pray...Dream...Write.

Day 15 Date: ____________

**John 1:3-5**

He created everything there is. Nothing exists that he didn't make. Life itself was in him, and this life gives light to everyone. The light shines through the darkness, and the darkness can never extinguish it. NLT

Read...Listen...Think...Talk/Pray...Dream...Write.

Day 16 Date: ____________

**John 1:14**
The Word became flesh and blood,
and moved into the neighborhood.
We saw the glory with our own eyes,
the one-of-a-kind glory,
like Father, like Son,
generous inside and out,
true from start to finish. MSG

Read...Listen...Think...Talk/Pray...Dream...Write.

Day 17 Date: ____________

**Psalm 1:2-3**

But his delight and desire are in the law of the Lord, and on His law (the precepts, the instructions, the teachings of God) he habitually meditates (ponders and studies) by day and by night. And he shall be like a tree firmly planted [and tended] by the streams of water, ready to bring forth its fruit in its season; its leaf also shall not fade or wither; and everything he does shall prosper [and come to maturity]. AMP

Read...Listen...Think...Talk/Pray...Dream...Write.

## Day 18 Date: ____________

**Psalm 8:1-9**

GOD, brilliant Lord, yours is a household name.
Nursing infants gurgle choruses about you;
toddlers shout the songs
That drown out enemy talk,
and silence atheist babble.
I look up at your macro-skies, dark and enormous,
your handmade sky-jewelry,
Moon and stars mounted in their settings.
Then I look at my micro-self and wonder,
Why do you bother with us?
Why take a second look our way?
Yet we've so narrowly missed being gods,
bright with Eden's dawn light.
You put us in charge of your handcrafted world,
repeated to us your Genesis-charge,
Made us lords of sheep and cattle,
even animals out in the wild,
Birds flying and fish swimming,
whales singing in the ocean deeps.
GOD, brilliant Lord, your name echoes around the world. MSG

Read...Listen...Think...Talk/Pray...Dream...Write.

Day 19 Date: ____________

**John 3:16-17**

This is how much God loved the world: He gave his Son, his one and only Son. And this is why: so that no one need be destroyed; by believing in him, anyone can have a whole and lasting life. God didn't go to all the trouble of sending his Son merely to point an accusing finger, telling the world how bad it was. He came to help, to put the world right again. MSG

Read...Listen...Think...Talk/Pray...Dream...Write.

Day 20 Date: ____________

**John 13:34-35**

So now I am giving you a new commandment: Love each other. Just as I have loved you, you should love each other. Your love for one another will prove to the world that you are my disciples. NLT

Read…Listen…Think…Talk/Pray…Dream…Write.

Day 21 Date: ____________

**Psalm 18:30-31**

Your way is perfect, LORD,
  and your word is correct.
You are a shield for those
  who run to you for help.
You alone are God!
  Only you are a mighty rock. CEV

Read...Listen...Think...Talk/Pray...Dream...Write.

Day 22 Date: ____________

**Psalm 18:32-33**

You give me strength
  and guide me right.
You make my feet run as fast
  as those of a deer,
  and you help me stand
  on the mountains. CEV

Read…Listen…Think…Talk/Pray…Dream…Write.

Day 23 Date: ____________

**Psalm 18:34-36**

You teach my hands to fight
  and my arms to use
  a bow of bronze.
You alone are my shield.
Your right hand supports me,
  and by coming to help me,
  you have made me famous.
You clear the way for me,
  and now I won't stumble. CEV

Read…Listen…Think…Talk/Pray…Dream…Write.

Day 24 Date: ____________

**John 14:12-14**

I tell you the truth. The person who believes in me will do the big work that I do. And he will do even bigger work because I go to my Father.

I will do anything you ask of my Father in my name. In that way the Son will make my Father's name great.

If you ask anything in my name, I will do it. WE

Read...Listen...Think...Talk/Pray...Dream...Write.

Day 25 Date: ____________

**John 16:23-24**

In that day you will no longer ask me anything. I tell you the truth, my Father will give you whatever you ask in my name. Until now you have not asked for anything in my name. Ask and you will receive, and your joy will be complete. NIV

Read...Listen...Think...Talk/Pray...Dream...Write.

Day 26 Date: ____________

**Jeremiah 1:4-8**

This is what GOD said: "Before I shaped you in the womb, I knew all about you. Before you saw the light of day, I had holy plans for you: A prophet to the nations—that's what I had in mind for you." But I said, "Hold it, Master GOD! Look at me. I don't know anything. I'm only a boy!" GOD told me, "Don't say, "I'm only a boy.' I'll tell you where to go and you'll go there. I'll tell you what to say and you'll say it. Don't be afraid of a soul. I'll be right there, looking after you." MSG

Read...Listen...Think...Talk/Pray...Dream...Write.

Day 27 Date: ____________

**Romans 1:16, 19, 20**

I am proud of the good news! It is God's powerful way of saving all people who have faith, whether they are Jews or Gentiles...They know everything that can be known about God, because God has shown it all to them. God's eternal power and character cannot be seen. But from the beginning of creation, God has shown what these are like by all he has made. That's why those people don't have any excuse. CEV

Read...Listen...Think...Talk/Pray...Dream...Write.

Day 28 Date: ____________

**Romans 8:28**

And we know that God causes all things to work together for good to those who love God, to those who are called according to His purpose. NASB

Read…Listen…Think…Talk/Pray…Dream…Write.

Day 29 Date: ____________

**Psalm 22:9-10**

You, LORD, brought me safely through birth, and you protected me when I was a baby at my mother's breast. From the day I was born, I have been in your care, and from the time of my birth, you have been my God. CEV

Read...Listen...Think...Talk/Pray...Dream...Write.

Day 30 Date: ____________

**Romans 8:31-32**

What then shall we say to these things? If God is for us, who can be against us? He who did not spare His own Son, but delivered Him up for us all, how shall He not with Him also freely give us all things? NKJV

Read...Listen...Think...Talk/Pray...Dream...Write.

Day 31 Date: ____________

**Romans 8:37-39**

None of this fazes us because Jesus loves us. I'm absolutely convinced that nothing—nothing living or dead, angelic or demonic, today or tomorrow, high or low, thinkable or unthinkable—absolutely nothing can get between us and God's love because of the way that Jesus our Master has embraced us. MSG

Read...Listen...Think...Talk/Pray...Dream...Write.

Day 32 Date: ___________

**Philippians 3:10**

[For my determined purpose is] that I may know Him [that I may progressively become more deeply and intimately acquainted with Him, perceiving and recognizing and understanding the wonders of His Person more strongly and more clearly], and that I may in that same way come to know the power outflowing from His resurrection [which it exerts over believers], and that I may so share His sufferings as to be continually transformed [in spirit into His likeness even] to His death....AMP

Read...Listen...Think...Talk/Pray...Dream...Write.

Day 33 Date: ____________

**Romans 12:1-2**

So here's what I want you to do, God helping you: Take your everyday, ordinary life—your sleeping, eating, going-to-work, and walking-around life—and place it before God as an offering. Embracing what God does for you is the best thing you can do for him. Don't become so well-adjusted to your culture that you fit into it without even thinking. Instead, fix your attention on God. You'll be changed from the inside out. Readily recognize what he wants from you, and quickly respond to it. Unlike the culture around you, always dragging you down to its level of immaturity, God brings the best out of you, develops well-formed maturity in you. MSG

Read...Listen...Think...Talk/Pray...Dream...Write.

Day 34 Date: ____________

**Psalm 25:4-5**

Show me Your ways, O LORD;
Teach me Your paths.
Lead me in Your truth and teach me,
For You are the God of my salvation;
On You I wait all the day. NKJV

Read…Listen…Think…Talk/Pray…Dream…Write.

Day 35 Date: ____________

**Psalm 25:6-7**

Remember, O LORD , your great mercy and love,
for they are from of old.
Remember not the sins of my youth
and my rebellious ways;
according to your love remember me,
for you are good, O LORD. NIV

Read…Listen…Think…Talk/Pray…Dream…Write.

Day 36 Date: ____________

**1 Corinthians 1:20, 25**

So where does this leave the philosophers, the scholars, and the world's brilliant debaters? God has made them all look foolish and has shown their wisdom to be useless nonsense...This "foolish" plan of God is far wiser than the wisest of human plans, and God's weakness is far stronger than the greatest of human strength. NLT

Read...Listen...Think...Talk/Pray...Dream...Write.

## Day 37 Date: ____________

**1 Corinthians 1:27-29**

But God chose things that look foolish to the people of the world. He has used those foolish things to put the wise people to shame. God chose the weak things to put to shame the strong people. And God chose the small things, things that people despise. Yes, he chose even the things which seem to be nothing. He did this to destroy the big things. He did this so that people would not be proud before God. WE

Read…Listen…Think…Talk/Pray…Dream…Write.

Day 38 Date: ____________

**Psalm 32:8, 10**

Let me give you some good advice;
I'm looking you in the eye
and giving it to you straight…
God—defiers are always in trouble;
GOD-affirmers find themselves loved
every time they turn around. MSG

Read…Listen…Think…Talk/Pray…Dream…Write.

Day 39 Date: ____________

**1 Corinthians 10:12-13**

So, if you think you are standing firm, be careful that you don't fall! No temptation has seized you except what is common to man. And God is faithful; he will not let you be tempted beyond what you can bear. But when you are tempted, he will also provide a way out so that you can stand up under it. NIV

Read...Listen...Think...Talk/Pray...Dream...Write.

Day 40 Date: ____________

**Psalm 34:9-10**
Honor the LORD!
You are his special people.
No one who honors the LORD
  will ever be in need.
Young lions may go hungry or even starve,
  but if you trust the LORD,
  you will never miss out
  on anything good. CEV

Read...Listen...Think...Talk/Pray...Dream...Write.

Day 41 Date: ____________

**2 Corinthians 5:17**

So if any one [be] in Christ, [there is] a new creation; the old things have passed away; behold all things have become new. Darby

Read...Listen...Think...Talk/Pray...Dream...Write.

Day 42 Date: ___________

**2 Corinthians 6:14-15**

Don't team up with those who are unbelievers. How can goodness be a partner with wickedness? How can light live with darkness? What harmony can there be between Christ and the Devil? How can a believer be a partner with an unbeliever? NLT

Read...Listen...Think...Talk/Pray...Dream...Write.

Day 43 Date: ____________

**Psalm 37:4**

Delight yourself in the LORD
and he will give you the desires of your heart. NIV

**Psalms 25:14**

Friendship with God is reserved for those who reverence him.
With them alone he shares the secrets of his promises. LB

Read…Listen…Think…Talk/Pray…Dream…Write.

Day 44 Date: ____________

**2 Corinthians 9:6-7**

Remember this—a farmer who plants only a few seeds will get a small crop. But the one who plants generously will get a generous crop. You must each make up your own mind as to how much you should give. Don't give reluctantly or in response to pressure. For God loves the person who gives cheerfully. NLT

Read...Listen...Think...Talk/Pray...Dream...Write.

Day 45 Date: ____________

**Galatians 2:20**

Christ's life showed me how, and enabled me to do it. I identified myself completely with him. Indeed, I have been crucified with Christ. My ego is no longer central. It is no longer important that I appear righteous before you or have your good opinion, and I am no longer driven to impress God. Christ lives in me. The life you see me living is not "mine," but it is lived by faith in the Son of God, who loved me and gave himself for me. MSG

Read…Listen…Think…Talk/Pray…Dream…Write.

## Day 46 Date: ____________

**Galatians 4:4-7**

But when the right time came, God sent his Son, born of a woman, subject to the law. God sent him to buy freedom for us who were slaves to the law, so that he could adopt us as his very own children. And because you Gentiles have become his children, God has sent the Spirit of his Son into your hearts, and now you can call God your dear Father. Now you are no longer a slave but God's own child. And since you are his child, everything he has belongs to you. NLT

Read...Listen...Think...Talk/Pray...Dream...Write.

Day 47 Date: ____________

**Galatians 6:9-10**

We must not get tired of doing good things. If we do not stop doing them, we will get something back when the right time comes. So then, when we can, we should do good to all people. But most of all, we should do it to those who are in God's family. WE

Read...Listen...Think...Talk/Pray...Dream...Write.

Day 48 Date: ______________

**Psalm 40:5**

Many, O LORD my God, are the wonders which You have done,
And Your thoughts toward us;
There is none to compare with You.
If I would declare and speak of them,
They would be too numerous to count. NASB

Read...Listen...Think...Talk/Pray...Dream...Write.

Day 49 Date: ____________

**Ephesians 3:14-19**

For this reason I kneel before the Father, from whom his whole family in heaven and on earth derives its name. I pray that out of his glorious riches he may strengthen you with power through his Spirit in your inner being, so that Christ may dwell in your hearts through faith. And I pray that you, being rooted and established in love, may have power, together with all the saints, to grasp how wide and long and high and deep is the love of Christ, and to know this love that surpasses knowledge—that you may be filled to the measure of all the fullness of God. NIV

Read...Listen...Think...Talk/Pray...Dream...Write.

Day 50 Date: ____________

**Ephesians 3:20-21**

Now to him who is able to do immeasurably more than all we ask or imagine, according to his power that is at work within us, to him be glory in the church and in Christ Jesus throughout all generations, for ever and ever! NIV

Read...Listen...Think...Talk/Pray...Dream...Write.

Day 51 Date: ____________

**Philippians 1:5-6**

I thank God for the joy we share in telling the good news from the very first day until now. God began to do a good work in you. And I am sure that he will keep on doing it until he has finished it. He will keep on until the day Jesus Christ comes again. WE

Read...Listen...Think...Talk/Pray...Dream...Write.

Day 52 Date: ____________

**Psalm 46:10**
Be still, and know that I am God;
I will be exalted among the nations,
I will be exalted in the earth! NKJV

**Psalm 37:7**
Be still before the LORD and wait patiently for him;
do not fret when men succeed in their ways,
when they carry out their wicked schemes. NIV

Read…Listen…Think…Talk/Pray…Dream…Write.

Day 53 Date: ____________

**Philippians 2:3-4**

Do nothing from selfishness or empty conceit, but with humility of mind regard one another as more important than yourselves; do not merely look out for your own personal interests, but also for the interests of others. NASB

Read…Listen…Think…Talk/Pray…Dream…Write.

Day 54 Date: ____________

**Philippians 3:12-14**

I'm not saying that I have this all together, that I have it made. But I am well on my way, reaching out for Christ, who has so wondrously reached out for me. Friends, don't get me wrong: By no means do I count myself an expert in all of this, but I've got my eye on the goal, where God is beckoning us onward—to Jesus. I'm off and running, and I'm not turning back. MSG

Read...Listen...Think...Talk/Pray...Dream...Write.

Day 55 Date: ____________

**Philippians 4:4-7**

Rejoice in the Lord always. I will say it again: Rejoice! Let your gentleness be evident to all. The Lord is near. Do not be anxious about anything, but in everything, by prayer and petition, with thanksgiving, present your requests to God. And the peace of God, which transcends all understanding, will guard your hearts and your minds in Christ Jesus. NIV

Read...Listen...Think...Talk/Pray...Dream...Write.

Day 56 Date: ____________

**Philippians 4:8-9**

Finally, brethren, whatever is true, whatever is honorable, whatever is right, whatever is pure, whatever is lovely, whatever is of good repute, if there is any excellence and if anything worthy of praise, dwell on these things. The things you have learned and received and heard and seen in me, practice these things, and the God of peace will be with you. NASB

Read...Listen...Think...Talk/Pray...Dream...Write.

Day 57 Date: ____________

**Philippians 4:11-12**

I am not complaining about having too little. I have learned to be satisfied with whatever I have. I know what it is to be poor or to have plenty, and I have lived under all kinds of conditions. I know what it means to be full or to be hungry, to have too much or too little. CEV

**Philippians 4:13, 19**

I can do all things through Him who strengthens me...And my God will supply all your needs according to His riches in glory in Christ Jesus. NASB

Read...Listen...Think...Talk/Pray...Dream...Write.

Day 58 Date: ____________

**Psalm 56:3-4**

When I am afraid,
  I will put my trust in You.
In God, whose word I praise,
  In God I have put my trust;
  I shall not be afraid.
  What can mere man do to me? NASB

Read...Listen...Think...Talk/Pray...Dream...Write.

Day 59 Date: ____________

**Colossians 1:9-13**

We have not stopped praying for you since the first day we heard about you. In fact, we always pray that God will show you everything he wants you to do and that you may have all the wisdom and understanding that his Spirit gives. Then you will live a life that honors the Lord, and you will always please him by doing good deeds. You will come to know God even better. His glorious power will make you patient and strong enough to endure anything, and you will be truly happy. I pray that you will be grateful to God for letting you have part in what he has promised his people in the kingdom of light. God rescued us from the dark power of Satan and brought us into the kingdom of his dear Son.... CEV

Read...Listen...Think...Talk/Pray...Dream...Write.

Day 60 Date: ____________

**Colossians 2:6-7**

Therefore as you have received Christ Jesus the Lord, so walk in Him, having been firmly rooted and now being built up in Him and established in your faith, just as you were instructed, and overflowing with gratitude. NASB

Read...Listen...Think...Talk/Pray...Dream...Write.

Day 61 Date: ____________

**Psalm 118:6**

The LORD is with me; I will not be afraid.
  What can man do to me? NIV

**Psalm 119:165**

Great peace have they who love Your law;
  nothing shall offend them or make them stumble. AMP

Read…Listen…Think…Talk/Pray…Dream…Write.

Day 62 Date: ____________

**Psalm 133:1**
How good and pleasant it is
when brothers live together in unity! NIV

**Psalm 135:6**
The LORD does whatever pleases him,
in the heavens and on the earth,
in the seas and all their depths. NIV

Read…Listen…Think…Talk/Pray…Dream…Write.

Day 63 Date: ____________

**Colossians 2:8-10**

Don't let anyone lead you astray with empty philosophy and high-sounding nonsense that come from human thinking and from the evil powers of this world, and not from Christ. For in Christ the fullness of God lives in a human body, and you are complete through your union with Christ. He is the Lord over every ruler and authority in the universe. NLT

Read...Listen...Think...Talk/Pray...Dream...Write.

Day 64 Date: ____________

**Psalm 119:9, 11**

How can a young man keep his way pure?
By keeping it according to Your word…
Your word I have treasured in my heart,
That I may not sin against You. NASB

Read…Listen…Think…Talk/Pray…Dream…Write.

Day 65 Date: ____________

**Colossians 3:15-17**

And let the peace (soul harmony which comes) from Christ rule (act as umpire continually) in your hearts [deciding and settling with finality all questions that arise in your minds, in that peaceful state] to which as [members of Christ's] one body you were also called [to live]. And be thankful (appreciative), [giving praise to God always]. Let the word [spoken by] Christ (the Messiah) have its home [in your hearts and minds] and dwell in you in [all its] richness, as you teach and admonish and train one another in all insight and intelligence and wisdom [in spiritual things, and as you sing] psalms and hymns and spiritual songs, making melody to God with [His] grace in your hearts. AMP

Read...Listen...Think...Talk/Pray...Dream...Write.

Day 66 Date: ____________

**Colossians 3:23-24**

Work hard and cheerfully at whatever you do, as though you were working for the Lord rather than for people. Remember that the Lord will give you an inheritance as your reward, and the Master you are serving is Christ. NLT

Read...Listen...Think...Talk/Pray...Dream...Write.

Day 67 Date: ____________

**Psalm 139:1-4**

O LORD, you have examined my heart
 and know everything about me.
You know when I sit down or stand up.
 You know my every thought when far away.
You chart the path ahead of me
 and tell me where to stop and rest.
 Every moment you know where I am.
You know what I am going to say
 even before I say it, LORD. NLT

Read...Listen...Think...Talk/Pray...Dream...Write.

Day 68 Date: ____________

**Psalm 139:5-8**

You both precede and follow me.
    You place your hand of blessing on my head.
Such knowledge is too wonderful for me,
    too great for me to know!
I can never escape from your spirit!
    I can never get away from your presence!
If I go up to heaven, you are there;
    if I go down to the place of the dead, you are there. NLT

Read…Listen…Think…Talk/Pray…Dream…Write.

Day 69 Date: ______________

**Psalm 139:9-12**

If I ride the wings of the morning,
if I dwell by the farthest oceans,
even there your hand will guide me,
and your strength will support me.
I could ask the darkness to hide me
and the light around me to become night—
but even in darkness I cannot hide from you.
To you the night shines as bright as day.
Darkness and light are both alike to you. NLT

Read…Listen…Think…Talk/Pray…Dream…Write.

Day 70 Date: ____________

**Psalm 139:13-16**

You made all the delicate, inner parts of my body
and knit me together in my mother's womb.
Thank you for making me so wonderfully complex!
Your workmanship is marvelous—and how well I know it.
You watched me as I was being formed in utter seclusion,
as I was woven together in the dark of the womb.
You saw me before I was born.
Every day of my life was recorded in your book.
Every moment was laid out
before a single day had passed. NLT

Read…Listen…Think…Talk/Pray…Dream…Write.

Day 71 Date: ____________

**Psalm 139:17-18, 23-24**

How precious are your thoughts about me, O God!
They are innumerable!
I can't even count them;
they outnumber the grains of sand!
And when I wake up in the morning,
you are still with me!...
Search me, O God, and know my heart;
test me and know my thoughts.
Point out anything in me that offends you,
and lead me along the path of everlasting life. NLT

Read...Listen...Think...Talk/Pray...Dream...Write.

Day 72 Date: ____________

**1 Thessalonians 5:16-18**

Always be joyful and never stop praying. Whatever happens, keep thanking God because of Jesus Christ. This is what God wants you to do. CEV

Read…Listen…Think…Talk/Pray…Dream…Write.

Day 73 Date: ____________

**1 Timothy 4:12**

Let no one despise or think less of you because of your youth, but be an example (pattern) for the believers in speech, in conduct, in love, in faith, and in purity. AMP

Read…Listen…Think…Talk/Pray…Dream…Write.

Day 74 Date: ____________

**Psalm 147:4-5, 11**

He determines the number of the stars
  and calls them each by name.
Great is our Lord and mighty in power;
  his understanding has no limit. …
The LORD delights in those who fear him,
  who put their hope in his unfailing love. NIV

Read…Listen…Think…Talk/Pray…Dream…Write.

Day 75 Date: ______________

**2 Timothy 1:7**
For God did not give us a spirit of timidity, but a spirit of power, of love and of self-discipline. NIV

**2 Timothy 2:3-7**
Endure hardship with us like a good soldier of Christ Jesus. No one serving as a soldier gets involved in civilian affairs—he wants to please his commanding officer. Similarly, if anyone competes as an athlete, he does not receive the victor's crown unless he competes according to the rules. The hardworking farmer should be the first to receive a share of the crops. Reflect on what I am saying, for the Lord will give you insight into all this. NIV

Read…Listen…Think…Talk/Pray…Dream…Write.

Day 76 Date: ____________

**Proverbs 3:5-6**

Trust in the LORD with all your heart,
  and do not lean on your own understanding.
In all your ways acknowledge him,
  and he will make straight your paths. ESV

Read…Listen…Think…Talk/Pray…Dream…Write.

Day 77 Date: ____________

**2 Timothy 3:14-15**

You, however, continue in the things you have learned and become convinced of, knowing from whom you have learned them, and that from childhood you have known the sacred writings which are able to give you the wisdom that leads to salvation through faith which is in Christ Jesus. NASB

Read…Listen…Think…Talk/Pray…Dream…Write.

Day 78 Date: ____________

**2 Timothy 3:16-17**

All Scripture is inspired by God and profitable for teaching, for reproof, for correction, for training in righteousness; so that the man of God may be adequate, equipped for every good work. NASB

Read…Listen…Think…Talk/Pray…Dream…Write.

Day 79 Date: ____________

**Proverbs 4:6-7, 23**

Do not forsake wisdom, and she will protect you;
love her, and she will watch over you.
Wisdom is supreme; therefore get wisdom.
Though it cost all you have, get understanding…
Above all else, guard your heart,
for it is the wellspring of life. NIV

Read…Listen…Think…Talk/Pray…Dream…Write.

Day 80 Date: ____________

**Hebrews 4:12-13**

For the word of God is full of living power. It is sharper than the sharpest knife, cutting deep into our innermost thoughts and desires. It exposes us for what we really are. Nothing in all creation can hide from him. Everything is naked and exposed before his eyes. This is the God to whom we must explain all that we have done. NLT

Read...Listen...Think...Talk/Pray...Dream...Write.

Day 81 Date: ____________

**Hebrews 4:14-16**

We have a great high priest, who has gone into heaven, and he is Jesus the Son of God. That is why we must hold on to what we have said about him. Jesus understands every weakness of ours, because he was tempted in every way that we are. But he did not sin! So whenever we are in need, we should come bravely before the throne of our merciful God. There we will be treated with undeserved kindness, and we will find help. CEV

Read...Listen...Think...Talk/Pray...Dream...Write.

Day 82 Date: ____________

**Proverbs 10:19**

When words are many, sin is not absent,
  but he who holds his tongue is wise. NIV

**Proverbs 11:12**

It's stupid to say bad things
  about your neighbors.
If you are sensible,
  you will keep quiet. CEV

Read...Listen...Think...Talk/Pray...Dream...Write.

Day 83 Date: ____________

**Proverbs 11:24-25**

One gives freely, yet grows all the richer;
  another withholds what he should give, and only suffers want.
Whoever brings blessing will be enriched,
  and one who waters will himself be watered. ESV

Read…Listen…Think…Talk/Pray…Dream…Write.

Day 84 Date: ____________

**Hebrews 11:1-3, 6**

The fundamental fact of existence is that this trust in God, this faith, is the firm foundation under everything that makes life worth living. It's our handle on what we can't see. The act of faith is what distinguished our ancestors, set them above the crowd. By faith, we see the world called into existence by God's word, what we see created by what we don't see...It's impossible to please God apart from faith. And why? Because anyone who wants to approach God must believe both that he exists and that he cares enough to respond to those who seek him. MSG

Read...Listen...Think...Talk/Pray...Dream...Write.

Day 85 Date: ____________

**Proverbs 12:11, 18**

Hard work means prosperity; only fools idle away their time.
Some people make cutting remarks, but the words of the wise bring healing. NLT

Read…Listen…Think…Talk/Pray…Dream…Write.

Day 86 Date: ____________

**Hebrews 12:1-3**

Therefore, since we have so great a cloud of witnesses surrounding us, let us also lay aside every encumbrance and the sin which so easily entangles us, and let us run with endurance the race that is set before us, fixing our eyes on Jesus, the author and perfecter of faith, who for the joy set before Him endured the cross, despising the shame, and has sat down at the right hand of the throne of God. For consider Him who has endured such hostility by sinners against Himself, so that you will not grow weary and lose heart. NASB

Read…Listen…Think…Talk/Pray…Dream…Write.

Day 87 Date: ______________

**James 1:2-4**
Consider it a sheer gift, friends, when tests and challenges come at you from all sides. You know that under pressure, your faith-life is forced into the open and shows its true colors. So don't try to get out of anything prematurely. Let it do its work so you become mature and well-developed, not deficient in any way. MSG

Read...Listen...Think...Talk/Pray...Dream...Write.

Day 88 Date: ____________

**Proverbs 12:25**
Worry weighs us down;
a cheerful word picks us up. MSG

**Proverbs 13:20**
Become wise by walking with the wise;
hang out with fools and watch your life fall to pieces. MSG

Read...Listen...Think...Talk/Pray...Dream...Write.

Day 89 Date: ____________

**James 1:5-8**

If you need wisdom—if you want to know what God wants you to do—ask him, and he will gladly tell you. He will not resent your asking. But when you ask him, be sure that you really expect him to answer, for a doubtful mind is as unsettled as a wave of the sea that is driven and tossed by the wind. People like that should not expect to receive anything from the Lord. They can't make up their minds. They waver back and forth in everything they do. NLT

Read...Listen...Think...Talk/Pray...Dream...Write.

Day 90 Date: ____________

**James 1:19-21**

My dear brothers, do not forget this. Every man should be quick to listen, slow to speak, and slow to be angry. When a man is angry, he does not do what God says is right. So stop all your dirty living. Stop doing so many wrong things. Listen quietly to the word that has been put in your hearts. It is able to save you. WE

Read…Listen…Think…Talk/Pray…Dream…Write.

Day 91 Date: ____________

**Proverbs 15:1, 22**

A gentle response defuses anger,
  but a sharp tongue kindles a temper-fire…
Refuse good advice and watch your plans fail;
  take good counsel and watch them succeed. MSG

Read…Listen…Think…Talk/Pray…Dream…Write.

Day 92 Date: ____________

**James 5:13-16**

If you are having trouble, you should pray. And if you are feeling good, you should sing praises. If you are sick, ask the church leaders to come and pray for you. Ask them to put olive oil on you in the name of the Lord. If you have faith when you pray for sick people, they will get well. The Lord will heal them, and if they have sinned, he will forgive them. If you have sinned, you should tell each other what you have done. Then you can pray for one another and be healed. The prayer of an innocent person is powerful, and it can help a lot. CEV

Read...Listen...Think...Talk/Pray...Dream...Write.

Day 93 Date: ____________

**1 Peter 5:6-7**

Therefore humble yourselves under the mighty hand of God, that He may exalt you in due time, casting all your care upon Him, for He cares for you. NKJV

Read...Listen...Think...Talk/Pray...Dream...Write.

Day 94 Date: ____________

**Proverbs 16:3, 9**

Commit your works to the LORD
And your plans will be established…
The mind of man plans his way,
But the LORD directs his steps. NASB

Read…Listen…Think…Talk/Pray…Dream…Write.

Day 95 Date: ____________

**2 Peter 1:3-4**

Everything that goes into a life of pleasing God has been miraculously given to us by getting to know, personally and intimately, the One who invited us to God. The best invitation we ever received! We were also given absolutely terrific promises to pass on to you—your tickets to participation in the life of God after you turned your back on a world corrupted by lust. MSG

Read...Listen...Think...Talk/Pray...Dream...Write.

Day 96 Date: ____________

**1 John 1:8-10**

If we say that we have not sinned, we are fooling ourselves, and the truth isn't in our hearts. But if we confess our sins to God, he can always be trusted to forgive us and take our sins away. If we say that we have not sinned, we make God a liar, and his message isn't in our hearts. CEV

Read...Listen...Think...Talk/Pray...Dream...Write.

Day 97 Date: ____________

**Proverbs 18:13, 21**

Answering before listening
  is both stupid and rude.
Words kill, words give life;
  they're either poison or fruit—you choose. MSG

Read...Listen...Think...Talk/Pray...Dream...Write.

Day 98 Date: ____________

**Proverbs 25:15**

With patience a ruler may be persuaded,
and a soft tongue will break a bone. ESV

**Proverbs 26:18-19**

Like a madman who throws firebrands, arrows, and death
is the man who deceives his neighbor
and says, "I am only joking!" ESV

Read…Listen…Think…Talk/Pray…Dream…Write.

Day 99 Date: ____________

**Proverbs 23:17-21**

Don't for a minute envy careless rebels;
soak yourself in the Fear-of-GOD-
That's where your future lies.
Then you won't be left with an armload of nothing.
Oh listen, dear child—become wise;
point your life in the right direction.
Don't drink too much wine and get drunk;
don't eat too much food and get fat.
Drunks and gluttons will end up on skid row,
in a stupor and dressed in rags. MSG

Read...Listen...Think...Talk/Pray...Dream...Write.

Day 100 Date: ____________

**Psalm 37:23-24**

The steps of a man are established by the LORD,
And He delights in his way.
When he falls, he will not be hurled headlong,
Because the LORD is the One who holds his hand. NASB

Read…Listen…Think…Talk/Pray…Dream…Write.

# References

Warren, Rick. *The Purpose Driven Life.* Grand Rapids: Zondervan Press, 2002.

Chambers, Oswald. *My Utmost for His Highest.* Uhrichsville: Barbour, 1935.

# About the Author

For most of his life Jeff's brothers have accused him of being a full time student. Too many years in school, eleven years working in the family business, and a dozen years in various forms of ministry are the make up of his career. Jeff has served in management, as a Pastor to college students, as an Associate Pastor, as a Senior Pastor and as an Executive Director of a start-up program for abandoned and neglected children.

Today, he is the Director of Upside Down Ministries, Inc. Upside Down Ministries is a non-profit organization that seeks to build and develop healthy relationships through writing, speaking, mentoring and conducting workshops.

He and his wife Libbi have been actively involved with Young Life as volunteer leaders and serving on a Young Life Committee. Jeff and Libbi have been married over 27 years. They have five children: Kristy, Billy, Dickson, Todd and Bo. Home is in Boone, North Carolina.

# Need a Speaker?

Click on **www.upsidedownministries.com** for more information about having Jeff Hendley speak to your group or hold a conference or workshop.

# Ordering Materials:

You can order materials through the website or contact Jeff Hendley...


Jeff Hendley
Upside Down Ministries, Inc.
PO Box 2567 • Boone, NC 28607
jeff@hendleys.net

www.ingramcontent.com/pod-product-compliance
Lightning Source LLC
Chambersburg PA
CBHW061959040426
42447CB00010B/1822
*9780976201403*